The Complete Ninja Creami Cookbook 2023

2000 Days of Fresh Recipes from Beginner to Expert for Making Ice Cream Mix-Ins, Sorbets, Smoothies and Shakers the Quickest and Easiest Way

Stephanie Karlee

Legal Notice:

Table of Contents

Introduction

Who doesn't like ice cream? Ice cream is undeniably one of the world's most popular frozen desserts. It's difficult to resist its sweet flavor, creamy texture, and refreshing coolness, as anyone can attest!

You may be surprised to learn that you can now start making your own ice cream at home. You can make your own ice cream at any time with Ninja Creami. You can also make smoothies, gelatos, sorbets, and milkshakes.

Don't make the mistake of assuming that the machine is costly or difficult to use. This is not true. This is one home appliance that is not only affordable but also a good investment. And, once you've read the instructions for operating, maintaining, and caring for it, you'll see that it's very simple to use.

It's not surprising, given that it comes from one of the world's leading kitchen appliance manufacturers. Ninja Kitchen has become well-known for producing a wide range of efficient and innovative kitchen appliances, including pressure cookers, air fryers, blenders, and many more.

Chapter 1:
- What is Ninja Creami and how it is work.

What is Ninja Creami?

Introducing the Ninja CREAMi, a cutting-edge new home ice cream maker that enables you to instantly convert frozen bases into ice cream, milkshakes, sorbets, and other frozen desserts. It would take hours to turn a uniformly frozen block into an extraordinarily smooth and creamy texture with other techniques, but thanks to the Ninja CREAMi's patented technology, it only takes minutes. "Creamify" is the name of this process. You have the option of using your base right away or freezing it for later use after it has undergone this metamorphosis.

The Benefits of Your Ninja CREAMi

Let's look at some of the Ninja CREAMi's special features and benefits.

- **Quick Processing Time:** To produce the creamiest, smoothest ice cream, sorbet, and gelato, the machine chums the ice cream mixture.
- **Simple to Create Multiple Flavors:** Start with a simple vanilla foundation and enjoy making two, three, or even six different flavors.
- **Make-Ahead Feature:** You can prepare as many different flavors of ice cream in advance and store them in the freezer for when you're ready to consume the CREAMi and process the base.
- **Easy to Clean:** Except for the part with the Dual Drive Motor, the Ninja CREAMi is dishwasher safe on the top rack. If you don't have a dishwasher, simply use warm water and soap to clean the parts.
- **Smaller Batch Size:** You won't need to keep a large ice cream container in your freezer because of the reduced batch size. Simply purchase additional pint containers and have an ice cream social or tasting party with as many different flavors as you'd like!
- **Ice Cream, Sorbet, and Light Ice Cream Modes:** Ice cream, gelato (Italian ice cream), sorbet (fruit or vegetable juice that has been frozen and treated), and light

ice cream may all be made at the touch of a button. Greater processing time at faster speeds is necessary to break up ice crystals and produce creamy sorbets and smoothie bowls, No matter what you want to prepare, the machine takes care of everything for you, so you don't have to do any guesswork.

Chapter 2:
- Ice cream recipes

1. Ice cream in the Philadelphia fashion

- Servings 4
- Prep: 5 Minutes / Freezing: 24 Hours

Ingredients

- 5 ml vanilla extract
- 6 oz heavy (whipping) cream
- 8 oz whole milk
- 0.5 oz cream cheese at room temperature
- 0.5 oz unsweetened cocoa powder
- 2 oz granulated sugar

Directions

1. In a large bowl that can be used in the microwave, microwave the cream cheese for 10 seconds. The cocoa powder, sugar, and vanilla extract should all be combined in a bowl; mix the ingredients together until frosting-like, about 60 seconds.
2. Add the heavy cream and milk to the mixture in a slow, steady stream once the sugar has completely dissolved.

3. Fill a CREAMi Pint that has been meticulously cleaned with the base. Place the container in the freezer for a full day while being covered with the storage lid.
4. Remove the cover from the CREAMi Pint and take it out of the freezer. Place the pint in the Ninja CREAM i's outer bowl, insert the Creamerizer TM Paddle into the lid, and make sure the lid assembly is securely fastened to the outside bowl. Move the lever to the right to raise the platform and secure it in place after setting the bowl assembly to rest on the motor base. Choose the "Ice Cream" function.
5. The ice cream in the pint needs to be taken out after the machine has finished its work. Serve immediately with your preferred toppings.

Nutrition:

- Kcal: 900 Fat: 58.9g Carbs: 74.0g

2. Caramel Ice Cream with Sea Salt

- Servings 4
- Prep: 5 Minutes / Cooking: 5 Minutes / Freezing: 24 Hours

Ingredients

- 2 oz whole milk
- 8 oz heavy cream
- 5 ml sea salt
- 4 large egg yolks
- 0.5 oz dark brown sugar
- 15 ml prepared caramel sauce.

Directions

1. A big basin of ice water should be prepared and set aside for subsequent usage.
2. A small pot should be used to whisk egg yolks, brown sugar, and caramel sauce until the sugar is dissolved and the mixture is well combined. Overheating shouldn't be used for this.
3. Stir with a whisk until the milk, heavy cream, and salt are all incorporated.
4. Continuously stir the mixture with a rubber spatula and continue cooking it until an instant-read thermometer registers between 165- and 175 degrees Fahrenheit.
5. Remove the pan from the heat and use a sieve with a fine screen to transfer the base into a CREAMi Pint. Be careful not to let any water spill into the base of the pint when placing it in the prepared ice water bath.
6. Place the storage cover on the pint container and freeze it for a full day after allowing the bottom to cool.
7. Remove the top from the CREAMi Pint and take it out of the freezer. Put the pint in the Ninja CREAMi's outer bowl, insert the Creamerizer TM Paddle into the lid, and make sure the lid assembly is securely fastened to the outside bowl. Having placed the.

Nutrition:

- Kcal: 720 Fat: 50.9g Carbs: 74.9g

Ingredients

- 6 oz heavy (whipping) cream
- 8 oz whole milk
- 2 oz mini chocolate chips (optional)
- 0.5 oz cream cheese at room temperature
- 2 oz granulated sugar
- 5 ml vanilla extract

Directions

1. In a large microwave-safe bowl, warm the cream cheese for 10 seconds. The mixture should be whisked for around 60 seconds or combined with a rubber spatula until it resembles frosting after the addition of the sugar and vanilla extract.
2. It takes some time to thoroughly mix the milk into the cream cheese and completely dissolve the sugar in the heavy cream before combining the cream cheese and sugar.
3. Fill a CREAMi Pint with the base after properly cleaning it. Place the container in the freezer for an entire day while it is covered with its storage lid.
4. Remove the top from the CREAMi Pint and take it out of the freezer. The pint container should be placed in the Ninja CREAMi's outer bowl. The outer bowl's lid should then be inserted into the Creamerizer TM Paddle, and the lid assembly should be secured to the outer bowl. After settling the bowl assembly on the motor base, elevate the platform and lock it in place by pulling the lever to the right. Select "Ice Cream" from the menu.
5. Remove the pint container's cap after the machine has finished processing it and set it aside. If you include chocolate chips, cut a 1.5-inch-wide hole in the pint and extend it all the way to the bottom using a spoon. It's perfectly natural for your treat's level to increase throughout this phase and go above the Max Fill line. Put the pint's lid back on, fill the opening with a quarter cup's worth of mini chocolate chips, and then choose the Mix-In setting on the machine.
6. Serve immediately with your preferred toppings.

Nutrition:

- Kcal: 890 Fat: 58.9g Protein: 11.9g

- Servings 4
- Prep: 5 Minutes / Cooking: 7 To 10 Minutes / Freezing: 24 Hours

Ingredients

- 2 oz whole milk
- 8 oz heavy (whipping) cream
- 5 ml vanilla extract
- 4 large egg yolks
- 0.5 oz light corn syrup
- 2 oz plus 0.5 oz granulated sugar

Directions

1. A big basin of ice water should be prepared and set aside for subsequent usage.
2. Combine the egg yolks, sugar, and corn syrup in a small saucepan. The ingredients should be well blended after being whisked together until the sugar has completely dissolved. This shouldn't involve overheating.
3. To assemble the ingredients, whisk in the milk, heavy cream, and vanilla extract.
4. Set the heat to medium and put the pan on the stove. Cook, often stirring with a rubber spatula, until an instant-read thermometer registers between 165 and 175 degrees Fahrenheit.
5. After turning off the heat, transfer the contents of the pan into a CREAMi Pint that has just been thoroughly cleaned. Place the container carefully into the newly-created ice water bath, being careful to keep water from getting into the base of the container.
6. The ice cream in the pint needs to be taken out once the machine has finished its work. Soon after cooking, serve.

Nutrition:

- Kcal: 1000 Fat: 58.9g Carbs: 74.9g

Ingredients

- 3 large egg yolks
- 2 oz whole milk
- 8 oz heavy cream
- 5 ml vanilla extract
- 0.5 oz plus 5 ml instant espresso powder
- 1 oz corn syrup
- 2 oz granulated sugar

Directions

1. A big basin of ice water should be prepared and set aside for subsequent usage.
2. In a small pot, add the sugar, corn syrup, egg yolks, and espresso powder. Stir constantly until the sugar dissolves and the mixture is thoroughly blended. This shouldn't involve overheating.
3. To assemble the ingredients, whisk in the milk, heavy cream, and vanilla extract.
4. Stirring frequently with a rubber spatula, cook the mixture until an instant-read thermometer reads 165 to 175 degrees Fahrenheit.
5. After turning off the heat, transfer the contents of the pan into a CREAMi Pint that has just been thoroughly cleaned. Taking care to keep water from getting into the container's base, carefully place the container in the ice water bath that has been made.
6. Set the storage cover over the
7. Take the ice cream out of the pint once the production procedure has been completed. Serve immediately with your preferred toppings.

Nutrition:

- Kcal: 900 Fat: 88.9g Carbs: 77.9g Protein: 31.9g

6. Peanut Butter Ice Cream

Ingredients

- 8 oz whole milk
- 2 oz granulated sugar
- 5 ml vanilla extract
- 6 oz heavy (whipping) cream
- 1 oz powdered peanut butter.

Directions

1. Blend the milk, sugar, vanilla extract, and peanut butter powder until completely creamy. Mix at high speed for a full minute.
2. The ingredients should be placed in a bowl of around medium size. Whip the heavy cream into the mixture.
3. Fill a CREAMi Pint with the base after properly cleaning it. Place the container in the freezer for an entire day while it is covered with its storage lid.
4. Remove the top from the CREAMi Pint and take it out of the freezer. Place the pint in the Ninja CREAMi's outer bowl, insert the CreamerizerTM Paddle into the lid, and make sure the cover assembly is securely fastened to the outside bowl. Move the lever to the right to raise the platform and secure it in place after setting the bowl assembly to rest on the motor base. Choose the "Ice Cream" function.
5. The ice cream in the pint needs to be taken out once the machine has finished its work. Soon after cooking, serve.

Nutrition:

- Kcal: 689 Fat: 58.9g Carbs: 37.9g Protein: 21.3g

Ingredients

- 5 ml golden syrup or corn syrup
- 5 ml freshly squeezed lemon juice.
- 8 oz heavy (whipping) cream
- 8 ounces fresh strawberries trimmed and quartered.
- 4 oz granulated sugar

Directions

1. In a big bowl, combine strawberries, sugar, golden syrup, and lemon juice. Use a potato masher or a fork to crush the strawberries until they are broken down but still have some lumps. After vigorously swirling the mixture for ten minutes, it is finished.
2. Use a rubber spatula to completely blend the ingredients in the bowl after adding the heavy cream.
3. Fill a CREAMi Pint with the base after properly cleaning it. Place the container in the freezer for an entire day while it is covered with its storage lid.
4. Remove the top from the CREAMi Pint and take it out of the freezer. Place the pint in the Ninja CREAMi's outer bowl, insert the CreamerizerTM Paddle into the lid, and make sure the cover assembly is securely fastened to the outside bowl. Move the lever to the right to raise the platform and secure it in place after setting the bowl assembly to rest on the motor base. Choose the "Ice Cream" function.
5. The ice cream in the pint needs to be taken out once the machine has finished its work. Serve immediately with your preferred toppings.

Nutrition:

- Kcal: 700 Fat: 45.9g Carbs: 44.9g Protein: 11.0g

8. Low-Sugar Vanilla Ice Cream

- Servings 4
- Prep: 10 Minutes / Freezing: 24 Hours

Ingredients

- 2 oz stevia cane sugar blend
- 5 ml vanilla extract
- 16 oz fat-free half-and-half

Directions

1. In a medium bowl, combine the sugar, vanilla, and half-and-half. Whisk until the sugar is completely dissolved. There will be bubbling in the mixture. Let it stand for at least five minutes, or until all the froth has dissipated.
2. Fill a CREAMi Pint with the base after properly cleaning it. Place the container in the freezer for an entire day while it is covered with its storage lid.
3. Remove the top from the CREAMi Pint and take it out of the freezer. Place the pint in the Ninja CREAMi's outer bowl, insert the CreamerizerTM Paddle into the lid, and make sure the cover assembly is securely fastened to the outside bowl. Move the lever to the right to raise the platform and secure it in place after setting the bowl assembly to rest on the motor base. Choose "Lite Ice Cream" as the function to utilize.
4. The ice cream in the pint needs to be taken out once the machine has finished its work. Soon after cooking, serve.

Nutrition:

- Kcal: 633 Fat: 58.9g Carbs: 74.9g Protein: 11.0g

- Servings 4
- Prep: 5 Minutes / Freezing: 24 Hours

Ingredients

- **2 oz** heavy (whipping) cream
- 4 oz plus 0.5 oz granulated sugar
- 4 oz frozen peas, thawed
- 8 oz whole milk
- 0.5 oz corn syrup
- 1 oz powdered peanut butter.
- 5 ml vanilla extract

Directions

1. Blend the peas with the milk, sugar, corn syrup, peanut butter powder, and vanilla extract until creamy.
2. Fill a CREAMi Pint with the base after properly cleaning it. The heavy cream should be whisked in all the way before being added. Place the container in the freezer for an entire day while it is covered with its storage lid.
3. Remove the top from the CREAMi Pint and take it out of the freezer. Place the pint inside the Ninja CREAMi's outer bowl and the CreamerizerTM Paddle inside the lid. Move the lever to the right to raise the platform and secure it in place after setting the bowl assembly to rest on the motor base. Choose the "Ice Cream" function.
4. The ice cream in the pint needs to be taken out once the machine has finished its work. Soon after cooking, serve.

Nutrition:

- Kcal: 300 Fat: 58.9g Carbs: 79.9g Protein: 5.8g

10. Chocolate Ice Cream

- Servings 4
- Prep: 5 Minutes / Freezing: 24 Hours

Ingredients

- 15 ml dark unsweetened cocoa powder
- 0.5 oz cream cheese at room temperature
- 2 oz granulated sugar
- 6 oz heavy cream
- 6 oz whole milk
- 8 oz frozen kale

Directions

1. Blend the frozen kale, cream cheese, sugar, chocolate, and milk until thoroughly combined.
2. Fill a CREAMi Pint with the base after properly cleaning it. The heavy cream should be whisked in all the way before being added. Place the container in the freezer for an entire day while it is covered with its storage lid.
3. The CREAMi Pint should be taken out of the freezer after the lid has been removed. After inserting the CreamerizerTM Paddle into the lid and the lid assembly into the outer bowl of the Ninja CREAMi, add the pint to the container. After positioning the bowl assembly so that it rests on the motor base, lift the platform and secure it in place by turning the lever to the right. Select "Ice Cream" from the menu.
4. The ice cream in the pint needs to be taken out once the machine has finished its work. Serve immediately with your preferred toppings.

Nutrition:

- Kcal: 470 Fat: 51.9g Carbs: 49.9g Protein: 4.4g

- Servings 4
- Prep: 5 Minutes / Freezing: 24 Hours

Ingredients

- 5 ml strawberry extract
- 8 oz frozen carrot slices, thawed.
- 4 oz trimmed and quartered fresh strawberries
- 4 oz heavy (whipping) cream
- 4 oz whole milk
- 0.5 oz cream cheese at room temperature
- **2 oz** granulated sugar
- 5 drops of red food coloring.

Directions

1. The carrots, strawberries, cream cheese, sugar, strawberry essence, milk, and food coloring should all be blended.
2. Fill a CREAMi Pint with the base after properly cleaning it. The heavy cream should be whisked in all the way before being added. Place the container in the freezer for an entire day while it is covered with its storage lid.
3. Remove the top from the CREAMi Pint and take it out of the freezer. Place the pint in the Ninja CREAMi's outer bowl, insert the CreamerizerTM Paddle into the lid, and make sure the cover assembly is securely fastened to the outside bowl. Turn the lever to the right to lift the platform and fix it in place after setting the bowl assembly so it sits on the motor base. Choose the "Ice Cream" function.
4. The ice cream in the pint needs to be taken out once the machine has finished its work. Serve immediately with your preferred toppings.

Nutrition:

- Kcal: 501 Fat: 65.9g Carbs: 14.9g Protein: 3.9g

12. Coconut-Vanilla Ice Cream

Ingredients

- Four oz organic sugar
- can of full-fat unsweetened coconut milk
- 5 ml vanilla extract

Directions

1. In a large bowl, mix the coconut milk, sugar, and vanilla until the sugar is completely dissolved.
2. Fill a CREAMi Pint with the base after properly cleaning it. Place the container in the freezer for an entire day while it is covered with its storage lid.
3. Remove the top from the CREAMi Pint and take it out of the freezer. Place the pint in the Ninja CREAMi's outer bowl, insert the CreamerizerTM Paddle into the lid, and make sure the cover assembly is securely fastened to the outside bowl. Turn the lever to the right to lift the platform and fix it in place after setting the bowl assembly so it sits on the motor base. Choose the "Ice Cream" function.
4. The ice cream in the pint needs to be taken out once the machine has finished its work. Serve immediately with your preferred toppings.

Nutrition:

- Kcal: 500 Fat: 48.6g Carbs: 64.7g Protein: 3.9g

13. Cotton Candy

Ingredients:

- 4 cups of ice cream base without vanilla
- 1 tsp. of Cotton Candy extract/flavor
- Blue food coloring

Instructions:

1. Combine all the ingredients. Add food coloring in 1 – 2 drop increments until the desired color is achieved. Light, pastel colors are best!
2. Adjust to desired taste.
3. Pour into an air-tight container and freeze for at least 6 hours.

Nutrition:

- Kcal: 430 Fat: 58.7g Carbs: 69.9g Protein: 2.9g

14. Lemon Ice cream Base

- Cooking Time: 10 minutes

Ingredients:

- 4 cups of ice cream base without vanilla
- 6 oz of lemon juice, chilled
- 5 tsp. of fresh lemon zest finely grated.

Instructions:

1. Mix each component together. Until a very pale yellow color is reached, keep adding food coloring.
2. To suit your tastes, adjust. If you want a stronger flavor, add extra lemon juice.
3. Pour into a container that can be sealed, then freeze for at least six hours.

Nutrition:

- Kcal: 780 Fat: 28.9g Carbs: 70.9g Protein: 11.9g

- Cooking Time: 10 minutes

Ingredients:

- 4 cups of heavy whipping cream, cold
- 4 cups of sweetened condensed milk, cold
- 4 tsp. of vanilla extract
- 2 vanilla bean pods, seeds

Instructions:

1. Beat the chilled whipping cream until it forms soft peaks.
2. Condensed milk should be added, and beating should continue until firm peaks form.
3. Add vanilla seeds and essence to the mixture.
4. Fill an airtight container with the mixture, then freeze it for at least six hours. ideally throughout night.
5. It will be necessary as the foundation for additional recipes in this book (without vanilla). Steps 1 - 3.

Nutrition:

- Kcal: 700 Fat: 23.9g Carbs: 44.9g Protein: 7.9g

- Cooking time: 10 minutes

Ingredients:

- 4 tbsp. of butter, room temperature
- 4 oz of granulated sugar
- 4 oz of heavy cream
- ½ tsp. of cinnamon

Instructions:

1. Melt the butter in a small, heavy-bottomed pot over medium heat.
2. Add the sugar and heavy cream and whisk with a wooden spoon or rubber spatula.
3. Don't stir the mixture as it boils. 4 to 5 minutes of boiling. Caramel sauce will thicken as it cools; do not wait for it to do so while it is still hot.
4. After removing the sauce from the heat, stir in the cinnamon. Transfer the caramel sauce to a glass container once it has cooled.
5. When the mixture boils, use a moist brush to remove sugar crystals from the pot's sides.

Nutrition:

- Kcal: 790 Fat: 43.9g Carbs: 56.9g Protein: 8.9g

- Cooking Time:

Ingredients:

- 24 oz of vanilla ice cream
- 1 box of cake/brownie mix – eggs, oil, and water needed according to package directions.
- 8 oz of whipped topping

Instructions:

1. Follow the instructions on the box to prepare the cake. Allow cooling to finish. ice overnight.
2. Before incorporating the ice cream into the cake, give it three minutes to sit. This will facilitate its spread.
3. Spread the whipped topping evenly over the ice cream layer.
4. for one to two more hours, freeze.

Nutrition:

- Kcal: 750 Fat: 50.9g Carbs: 74.9g Protein: 9.9g

18. Pumpkin Cheesecake Ice Cream

Ingredients:

- 8 oz. cream cheese
- 8 oz heavy cream
- 2 oz pumpkin puree
- 4 oz brown sugar
- 5 ml vanilla extract
- 2.5 ml pumpkin pie spice

Method:

1. Put the cream cheese in a bowl that can go in the microwave.
2. 30 seconds in the microwave.
3. The remaining ingredients should be added to the bowl.
4. Mix thoroughly.
5. Transfer to the pint container for Ninja Creami.
6. Freeze for 24 hours.
7. Process in the machine using the Ice Cream function.

19. Mocha & Nut Ice Cream

Ingredients:

- 1 6 ozs coconut cream
- 4 oz mocha cappuccino mix
- 15 ml raw agave nectar

Method:

1. In the Ninja Creami pint container, combine all the ingredients.
2. For 24 hours, freeze.
3. Include the container in the device.
4. Select Ice Cream function.

Ingredients:

- 15 ml cream cheese, softened.
- 8 oz whole milk
- 6 oz heavy cream
- 3 oz granulated sugar.

Mix-Ins

- 15 ml potato chips
- 15 ml mini pretzels
- 1 sugar cone, crushed.

Method:

1. Cream cheese should be microwaved for 10 seconds.
2. Add the sugar, cream, and milk by stirring.
3. Mix thoroughly.
4. Fill your Ninja Creami pint container with the mixture.
5. For 24 hours, freeze.
6. Move the container over to the device.
7. Push the Ice Cream button.

21. Cookie & Cream with Mint Ice Cream

Ingredients:

- 6 oz coconut cream
- 5 drops green food coloring.
- 30 ml raw agave nectar
- 8 oz oat milk
- 2 oz monk fruit sweetener
- 2.5 ml mint extract

Mix-in

- 3 chocolate sandwich cookies, sliced into quarters.

Method:

1. Whisk the coconut cream until smooth.
2. Stir in the rest of the ingredients except the mix-in.
3. Transfer the mixture to the Ninja Creami pint container.
4. Freeze for 24 hours.
5. Process in the machine using the Ice Cream function.
6. Add the chocolate sandwich cookie slices.
7. Process using the Mix-in mode.

22. Peanut Butter & Jelly Ice Cream

Ingredients:

- 4 egg yolks
- 15 ml sugar
- 3 oz heavy cream
- 8 oz whole milk
- 2 oz peanut butter
- 15 ml grape jelly

Method:

1. To a saucepan, add all the ingredients.
2. Completely combine by blending.
3. Set the pot over a medium heat source.
4. Cook the dish with constant stirring until the internal temperature reaches 165 degrees Fahrenheit.
5. Strain the mixture.
6. Let cool for 30 minutes.
7. Once cooled, transfer to the Ninja Creami pint container.
8. Freeze for 24 hours.
9. Place in the machine.

23. Blueberry Cheesecake Ice Cream

Ingredients:

- 4 egg yolks
- 15 ml granulated sugar
- 5 ml vanilla extract
- 15 ml blueberry preserves.
- 2 oz cream cheese
- 8 oz milk
- 3 oz heavy cream

Method:

1. To a saucepan, add all the ingredients.
2. Mix thoroughly.
3. Set the pan over a medium heat source.
4. Cook until the temperature has reached 165 degrees F, stirring constantly.
5. Strain the mixture.
6. Let cool for 30 minutes.
7. Once cooled, transfer to the Ninja Creami pint container.
8. Freeze for 24 hours.
9. Put the container in the machine.
10. Select the Ice Cream function.

- Preparation Time: 5 minutes
- Freeze Time: 24 hours
- Servings: 4

Ingredients:

- 30 ml monk fruit sweetener
- 30 ml raw agave nectar
- 8 oz milk
- 6 oz heavy cream
- 2.5 ml raspberry extract
- ¼ teaspoon lemon extract
- 2.5 ml vanilla extract
- 2 drops red or pink food coloring

Method:

1. In the pint container for Ninja Creami, combine all the ingredients.
2. For 24 hours, freeze.
3. Move the container over to the device.
4. select "Ice Cream" from the menu.

Chapter 3:
- Ice cream mix-ins recipes

25. Yummy Chocolate Coconut Ingredients:

- 14-ounce can full-fat unsweetened coconut milk
- 2 oz unsweetened almond milk
- 4 oz organic sugar
- 5 ml vanilla extract
- 30 ml toasted almond halves.
- 30 ml vegan chocolate chips

Method:

1. The coconut milk, almond milk, sugar, and vanilla should all be combined and the sugar should be dissolved in a medium bowl.
2. Fill a CREAMi Pint with the base. For 24 hours, freeze the container with the storage lid on.
3. Take the pint out of the freezer, then remove the lid. Put the pint in the Ninja® CREAMiTM's outer bowl, insert the CreamerizerTM Paddle into the lid, and secure the lid assembly to the outside bowl. Place the bowl assembly on the motor base, then elevate the platform and lock it in place by turning the handle to the right. Decide to use the Ice Cream feature.
4. Remove the pint container's lid once the machine has done processing.

26. Appetizing Coffee and Cookies Ice Cream

Ingredients:

- 15 ml cream cheese, at room temperature
- 2 oz granulated sugar
- 5 ml vanilla extract
- 15 ml instant espresso
- 6 oz heavy (whipping) cream
- 8 oz whole milk
- 2 oz crushed chocolate sandwich cookies

Method:

1. In a large bowl, combine the cream cheese, sugar, and vanilla. Beat the ingredients for about a minute, or until the mixture resembles frosting.
2. Slowly whisk in the milk, instant espresso, and heavy cream to create a smooth consistency.
3. A CREAMi Pint should be full of the base. For a full day, freeze the container with the cover on.
4. Before removing the cover, take the pint out of the freezer. Put the pint in the Ninja® CREAMiTM's outer bowl, insert the lid's CreamerizerTM Paddle, and secure the lid assembly to the outside bowl. Lift the platform after attaching the bowl assembly to the motor base, then lock it in place by pulling the lever to the right. Use the Ice Cream feature after choosing it.
5. Once the machine has finished processing, take off the pint container's lid. Make a hole in the pint's bottom using a spoon that is 112 inches wide. Replace the cover, put the crumbled cookies in the hole, and then select the Mix-In option.
6. Remove the ice cream from the pint once the machine has done processing. Serve right away.
7. Cooking and preparation advice: Be careful not to over-whisk the instant espresso because doing so could produce a lot of froth.

27. Vanilla Birthday Cake Ice Cream

Ingredients:

- 5 large egg yolks
- 2 oz corn syrup
- 2½ tablespoons granulated sugar
- 2 oz whole milk
- 8 oz heavy (whipping) cream
- 1½ tablespoons vanilla extract
- 15 ml vanilla cake mix
- 30 ml rainbow-colored sprinkles

Method:

1. The egg yolks, corn syrup, and sugar should all be blended and the sugar completely dissolved in a small pot. Never do this while it is hot. Add the milk, heavy cream, and vanilla after whisking. Set the pan over a medium heat source. Cook, using a rubber spatula to stir continuously, until an instant-read thermometer register 165°F to 175°F. After taking the pan off the heat, pour the base into a fresh CREAMER.
2. Stir in the vanilla cake mix until mixed once the base is cool enough to handle. Place the storage lid on the pint container, then place it in the freezer for 24 hours.
3. Before removing the cover, take the pint out of the freezer. Put the pint in the Ninja® CREAMiTM's outer bowl, insert the lid's CreamerizerTM Paddle, and secure the lid assembly to the outside bowl. Lift the platform after attaching the bowl assembly to the motor base, then lock it in place by pulling the lever to the right. Use the Ice Cream feature after choosing it.
4. Remove the cover from the pint container after the machine has done processing. Use a 112 inch wide spoon to poke a hole in the bottom of the pint. During this phase, it won't matter if your treat crosses the Max Fill line. Replace the top, fill the pint hole with the rainbow sprinkles, and then choose Mix-In.
5. Remove the ice cream from the pint once the machine has done processing. Serve right away.
6. The temperature must be maintained between 165°F and 175°F when cooking otherwise the ingredients will be overdone and the eggs will curdle (also known as get scrambled).

28. Homemade Cinnamon Cereal Milk Ice Cream

Ingredients:

- 4 large egg yolks
- 15 ml light corn syrup
- 2 oz plus 15 ml granulated sugar
- 2 oz whole milk
- 8 oz heavy (whipping) cream
- 5 ml vanilla extract
- 34 ozs cinnamon square cereal, divided

Method:

1. Set aside a sizable basin that has been filled with ice water.
2. The egg yolks, corn syrup, and sugar should all be blended and the sugar completely dissolved in a small pot. Never do this while it is hot.
3. Add the milk, heavy cream, and vanilla after whisking.
4. Set the pan over a medium heat source. Cook, using a rubber spatula to stir continuously, until an instant-read thermometer registers 165°F to 175°F. Add three cups of cereal after turning off the heat in the pan. For 20 minutes, let steep.
5. After taking the pan off the heat, pour the base into a fresh CREAMi Pint after passing it through a fine-mesh sieve. Make sure the water doesn't run into the base when you carefully place the container in the ready ice water bath.
6. After the base has cooled, cover it with the storage lid and freeze it for 24 hours.
7. Take the pint out of the freezer, then remove the lid. Put the pint in the Ninja® CREAMiTM's outer bowl, insert the CreamerizerTM Paddle into the lid, and secure the lid assembly to the outside bowl. Place the bowl assembly on the motor base, then elevate the platform and lock it in place by turning the handle to the right. Decide to use the Ice Cream feature.
8. Remove the lid from the pint container once the machine has done processing. Make a hole with a spoon that is 112 inches wide and reaches the pint's bottom. It is acceptable for your treat to go above the Max Fill line during this process. Replace the lid, add the last 2 oz of cereal to the pint's hole, and then choose the Mix-In option.
9. When the ice cream has finished processing, take it from the pint. Serve right away.

29. Extreme Triple-Chocolate Ice Cream

Ingredients:

- 4 large egg yolks
- 2 oz granulated sugar
- 15 ml unsweetened cocoa powder
- 15 ml hot fudge sauce
- 6 oz heavy (whipping) cream
- 4 oz whole milk
- 5 ml vanilla extract
- 2 oz white chocolate chips

Method:

1. Set aside a sizable basin that has been filled with ice water.
2. The egg yolks, sugar, and cocoa powder should all be blended and the sugar completely dissolved in a small pot. Never do this while it is hot.
3. Add the hot fudge, heavy cream, milk, and vanilla after whisking.
4. Set the pan over a medium heat source. Cook, using a rubber spatula to stir continuously, until an instant-read thermometer registers 165°F to 175°F.
5. After taking the pan off the heat, pour the base into a fresh CREAMi Pint after passing it through a fine-mesh sieve. Make sure the water doesn't run into the base when you carefully place the container in the ready ice water bath.
6. After the base has cooled, cover it with the storage lid and freeze it for 24 hours.
7. Remove the pint from the freezer before removing the lid. Place the pint in the outer bowl of the Ninja® CREAMiTM, slide the CreamerizerTM Paddle into the lid, and fasten the lid assembly to the outside bowl. After mounting the bowl assembly on the motor base, raise the platform, then lock it in place by moving the handle to the right. Select the Ice Cream function and utilize it.
8. Once the machine has finished processing, take off the pint container's lid. Make a hole in the pint's bottom using a spoon that is 112 inches wide. Your treat may cross the Max Fill line throughout this process without consequence. the pint's hole with the white chocolate chips, replace the top, and
9. Remove the ice cream from the pint once the machine has done processing. Serve right away with chosen garnishes.

30. Classic Bourbon-Maple-Walnut Ice Cream

Ingredients:

- 4 large egg yolks
- 2 oz maple syrup
- 2 oz corn syrup
- 30 ml bourbon
- 4 oz whole milk
- 8 oz heavy (whipping) cream
- 2 oz toasted walnut halves

Method:

1. Set aside a sizable basin that has been filled with ice water.
2. The egg yolks, maple syrup, corn syrup, and bourbon should all be thoroughly mixed in a small skillet. Never do this while it is hot.
3. Add the milk and heavy cream by whisking.
4. Set the pan over a medium heat source. Cook, using a rubber spatula to stir continuously, until an instant-read thermometer registers 165°F to 175°F.
5. Pour the base into a fresh CREAMi Pint after taking the pan off the heat. Make sure the water doesn't run into the base when you carefully place the container in the ready ice water bath.
6. After the base has cooled, cover it with the storage lid and freeze it for 24 hours.
7. Take the pint out of the freezer, then remove the lid. Put the pint in the Ninja® CREAMiTM's outer bowl, insert the CreamerizerTM Paddle into the lid, and secure the lid assembly to the outside bowl. After mounting the bowl assembly on the motor base, raise the platform, then lock it in place by moving the handle to the right. Select the Ice Cream function and utilize it.
8. Once the machine has finished processing, take off the pint container's lid. Make a hole in the pint's bottom using a spoon that is 112 inches wide. Your treat may cross the Max Fill line throughout this process without consequence. Replace the lid, add the roasted walnuts to the pint hole, and then select Mix-In.
9. Remove the ice cream from the pint once the machine has done processing. Serve right away.

31. Delectable Cookies and Coconut Ice Cream

Ingredients:

- 14-ouncecan full-fat unsweetened coconut milk
- 4 oz organic sugar
- 5 ml vanilla extract
- 4 chocolate sandwich cookies, crushed

Method:

1. Coconut milk, sugar, and vanilla should all be thoroughly blended and the sugar should be dissolved.
2. Fill a CREAMi Pint with the base. For 24 hours, freeze the container with the storage lid on.
3. Take the pint out of the freezer, then remove the lid. Put the pint in the Ninja® CREAMiTM's outer bowl, insert the CreamerizerTM Paddle into the lid assembly to the outside bowl and fasten it there. After mounting the bowl assembly on the motor base, raise the platform, then lock it in place by moving the handle to the right. Select the Ice Cream function and utilize it.
4. Once the machine has finished processing, take off the pint container's lid. Make a hole in the pint's bottom using a spoon that is 112 inches wide. Your treat may cross the Max Fill line throughout this process without consequence. After replacing the lid and adding the broken cookies to the pint, select the Mix-In option.
5. Remove the ice cream from the pint once the machine has done processing. Serve right away with chosen garnishes.

32. Minty Chip Ice Cream

- Serving: 4

Ingredients:

- 3 large egg yolks
- 15 ml corn syrup
- 2 oz granulated sugar
- 2 oz whole milk
- 6 oz heavy (whipping) cream

- 8 oz packed fresh spinach
- 4 oz frozen peas, thawed
- 5 ml mint extract
- 2 oz semisweet chocolate chips

Method:

1. Set aside a sizable basin that has been filled with ice water.
2. The egg yolks, corn syrup, and sugar should all be blended and the sugar completely dissolved in a small pot. Never do this while it is hot.
3. Add the milk and heavy cream by whisking.
4. Set the pan over a medium heat source. Cook, using a rubber spatula to stir continuously, until an instant-read thermometer registers 165°F to 175°F.
5. Pour the base into a fresh CREAMi Pint after taking the pan off the heat. Make sure the water doesn't run into the base when you carefully place the container in the ready ice water bath.
6. Set aside a sizable basin that has been filled with ice water.
7. The egg yolks, corn syrup, and sugar should all be blended and the sugar completely dissolved in a small pot. Never do this while it is hot.
8. Add the milk and heavy cream by whisking.
9. Set the pan over a medium heat source. Cook, using a rubber spatula to stir continuously, until an instant-read thermometer registers 165°F to 175°F.
10. Pour the base into a fresh CREAMi Pint after taking the pan off the heat. Make sure the water doesn't run into the base when you carefully place the container in the ready ice water bath.
11. Remove the lid from the pint container once the machine has done processing. Make a hole with a spoon that is 112 inches wide and reaches the pint's bottom. It is acceptable for your treat to go above the Max Fill line during this process. Replace the lid, add the chocolate chips to the pint's hole, and then choose the Mix-In option.
12. Remove the ice cream from the pint once the machine has done processing. Serve right away.

33. Fresh Coconut Mint Chip Ice Cream

- Serving: 4

Ingredients:

- 14-ouncecan full-fat unsweetened coconut milk
- 4 oz organic sugar
- 2.5 ml mint extract
- 2 oz mini vegan chocolate chips

Method:

1. Whisk the coconut milk, sugar, and mint flavoring together in a medium bowl until the sugar has completely dissolved.
2. Fill a CREAMi Pint with the base. For 24 hours, freeze the container with the storage lid on.
3. Before removing the cover, take the pint out of the freezer. Put the pint in the Ninja® CREAMiTM's outer bowl, insert the lid's CreamerizerTM Paddle, and secure the lid assembly to the outside bowl. Place the bowl assembly on the motor base, then raise the platform and secure it in position by turning the handle to the right. Use the Ice Cream feature after choosing it.
4. Remove the cover from the pint container after the machine has done processing. Use a 112 inch wide spoon to poke a hole in the bottom of the pint. During this phase, it won't matter if your treat crosses the Max Fill line. Before removing the cover, take the pint out of the freezer. Put the pint in the Ninja® CREAMiTM's outer bowl, insert the lid's CreamerizerTM Paddle, and secure the lid assembly to the outside bowl. Place the bowl assembly on the motor base, then raise the platform and secure it in position by turning the handle to the right. Use the Ice Cream feature after choosing it.
5. Remove the pint container's lid once the machine has done processing. Use a spoon that is 112 inches wide to make a hole in the bottom of the pint. During this phase, your treat may go above the Max Fill line without any negative effects. Prior to removing the top, remove the pint from the freezer. In the Ninja® CREAMiTM, insert the pint into the outer bowl, slide the CreamerizerTM Paddle into the lid, and secure the lid assembly to the outside bowl. To lift the platform and secure it in position, set the bowl assembly on the motor base and turn the handle to the right. Utilize the Ice Cream feature by choosing it.
6. Remove the cover from the pint container after the machine has done processing. Use a 112 inch wide spoon to poke a hole in the bottom of the pint. During this phase, it won't matter if your treat crosses the Max Fill line. Incorporate the micro chocolate chips into the pint's hole, replace the top, and then select the Mix-In menu item.
7. Once the machine has finished processing, remove the ice cream from the pint. Serve immediately with the selected garnishes.

- Serving: 4

Ingredients:

- 8 oz canned pureed sweet potato
- 15 ml corn syrup
- 2 oz plus 15 ml light brown sugar
- 5 ml vanilla extract
- 5 ml cinnamon
- 6 oz heavy cream
- 2 oz mini marshmallows

Method:

1. Blend the sweet potato puree with the corn syrup, brown sugar, cinnamon, vanilla, and sugar. Blend until smooth on high.
2. Fill a CREAMi Pint with the base. Add the heavy cream and blend by whisking. For 24 hours, freeze the container with the storage lid on.
3. Take the pint out of the freezer, then remove the lid. Put the pint in the Ninja® CREAMiTM's outer bowl, insert the CreamerizerTM Paddle into the lid, and secure the lid assembly to the outside bowl. Place the bowl assembly on the motor base, then elevate the platform and lock it in place by turning the handle to the right. Decide to use the Ice Cream feature.
4. Remove the lid from the pint container once the machine has done processing. Make a hole with a spoon that is 112 inches wide and reaches the pint's bottom. It is acceptable for your treat to go above the Max Fill line during this process. Replace the lid, place the marshmallows in the pint's hole, and then choose the Mix-In option.
5. Remove the ice cream from the pint once the machine has done processing. Serve right away with chosen garnishes.

Chapter 4:
- Smoothie recipes

35. Bowl of almond smoothie

- Serves 1

Ingredients

- 1½ frozen ripe bananas
- 2 oz vanilla or chocolate almond milk
- 2 oz cold brew coffee
- 0.5 oz unsweetened almond butter
- 0.5 oz cocoa powder

Instructions

1. In a big bowl, add banana, almond milk, coffee that has been brewed, almond butter, and chocolate powder.
2. Fill a Ninja CREAMi Dessert Tub with the mixture.
3. Frozen for 24 hours with the lid on the tub.
4. Remove the cover off the tub and put it in the outer bowl after the 24-hour period has passed. Put the Creamerizer Paddle in place.
5. Lock the Outer Bowl into position on the motor base.
6. The machine can be started by pressing the power button.
7. then select smoothie bowl from the menu.
8. Release the outer bowl from the motor base once it has been finished. Take off the lid.

Nutrition:

- Kcal:179 Carbs:10g Fat:11g Protein:2g

- Serves 2

INGREDIENTS

- 4 oz water
- 2 oz quick oats
- 8 oz Greek vanilla yogurt
- 4 oz sliced banana
- 15 ml honey

Instructions

1. Oatmeal and water should be combined in a small microwave-safe bowl. Microwave on high for approximately one minute.
2. After removing the bowl from the microwave, thoroughly blend it with the yogurt, banana, and honey.
3. Fill a Ninja CREAMi Dessert Tub with the mixture.
4. Frozen for 24 hours with the lid on the tub.
5. Remove the cover off the tub and put it in the outer bowl after the 24-hour period has passed. Put the Creamerizer Paddle in place.
6. Lock the Outer Bowl into position on the motor base.
7. The machine can be started by pressing the power button.
8. then select smoothie bowl from the menu.
9. Release the outer bowl from the motor base once it has been finished. Take off the lid.

Nutrition:

- Kcal:171 Carbs:2g Fat:5g Protein:4g

37. Strawberry Smoothie Bowl

- Serves 2

Ingredients

- 1 oz vanilla protein powder
- 2 oz agave nectar
- 2 oz pineapple juice
- 4 oz whole milk
- 8 oz ripe banana, cut into pieces.
- 8 oz fresh strawberries chopped.

Instructions

1. In a large bowl, add the protein powder, agave nectar, pineapple juice, and milk. Whisk to thoroughly blend.
2. Use the back of a spoon to firmly press the banana and strawberry into a Ninja CREAMi Dessert Tub below the maximum fill line.
3. Add the milk mixture on top and whisk to blend.
4. Frozen for 24 hours with the lid on the tub.
5. Remove the cover off the tub and put it in the outer bowl after the 24-hour period has passed. Put the Creamerizer Paddle in place.
6. Lock the Outer Bowl into position on the motor base.
7. The machine can be started by pressing the power button.
8. then select smoothie bowl from the menu.
9. Release the outer bowl from the motor once it is finished.
10. Serve and enjoy!

Nutrition:

- Kcal:168 Carbs:9g Fat:17g Protein:10g

38. Raspberry Smoothie Bowl

- Serves 2

Ingredients

- 8 oz brewed coffee.
- 4 oz oat milk
- 1 oz almond butter
- 8 oz fresh raspberries
- 1 large, sliced banana.

Instructions

1. Place all ingredients in a high-speed blender, and blend until combined and creamy.
2. Fill a Ninja CREAMi Dessert Tub with the mixture.
3. Frozen for 24 hours with the lid on the tub.
4. Remove the cover off the tub and put it in the outer bowl after the 24-hour period has passed. Put the Creamerizer Paddle in place.
5. Lock the Outer Bowl into position on the motor base.
6. The machine can be started by pressing the power button.
7. then select smoothie bowl from the menu.
8. Release the outer bowl from the motor base once it has been finished. Take off the lid.
9. Serve and enjoy!

Nutrition:

- Kcal:178 Carbs:7g Fat:15.0g Protein:1.9g

- Serves 2

Ingredients

- Six oz fresh strawberries chopped
- 6 oz fresh raspberries
- Six oz fresh blueberries
- 6 oz fresh blackberries
- 2 oz plain Greek yogurt
- 0.5 oz honey

Instructions

1. Place the berries in a Ninja CREAMi Dessert Tub and, using the back of a spoon, firmly press them down to the maximum fill line.
2. Mix in the yogurt and honey.
3. Frozen for 24 hours with the lid on the tub.
4. Remove the cover off the tub and put it in the outer bowl after the 24-hour period has passed. Put the Creamerizer Paddle in place.
5. Lock the Outer Bowl into position on the motor base.
6. The machine can be started by pressing the power button.
7. then select smoothie bowl from the menu.
8. Once it is done, release the Outer bowl from the motor base. Remove the lid.
9. Serve and enjoy!

Nutrition:

- Kcal:190 Carbs:9.9g Fat:17g Protein:1.0g

- serves 2

Ingredients

- 8 oz cranberry juice
- 2 oz agave syrup
- 8 oz frozen cherry and berry mix

Instructions

1. In a big bowl, add the cranberry juice, agave syrup, and stir to blend.
2. Fill a Ninja CREAMi Dessert Tub with the cherry and berry mixture.
3. Add the cocktail mixture on top and mix well.
4. Frozen for 24 hours with the lid on the tub.
5. Remove the cover off the tub and put it in the outer bowl after the 24-hour period has passed. Put the Creamerizer Paddle in place.
6. Lock the Outer Bowl into position on the motor base.
7. The machine can be started by pressing the power button.
8. then select smoothie bowl from the menu.
9. Release the outer bowl from the motor base once it has been finished. Take off the lid.
10. Serve and enjoy!

Nutrition:

- Kcal:180 Carbs:8g Fat:13g Protein:11g

41. Pineapple Smoothie Bowl

- Serves 2

Ingredients

- 2 ripe bananas, cut into pieces.
- 8 oz fresh pineapple chopped.
- 2 oz yogurt
- 1 oz honey

Instructions

1. Add all ingredients to a large bowl and stir to thoroughly incorporate.
2. Fill a Ninja CREAMi Dessert Tub with the mixture.
3. Frozen for 24 hours with the lid on the tub.
4. Remove the cover off the tub and put it in the outer bowl after the 24-hour period has passed. Put the Creamerizer Paddle in place.
5. Lock the Outer Bowl into position on the motor base.
6. The machine can be started by pressing the power button.
7. then select smoothie bowl from the menu.
8. Release the outer bowl from the motor base once it has been finished. Take off the lid.
9. Serve and enjoy!

Nutrition:

- Kcal:177 Carbs:7.9g Fat:12g Protein:1.3g

- serves 2

Ingredients

- 6 oz frozen mango pieces
- 4 oz frozen raspberries
- 4 oz of Greek yogurt
- 1 oz of avocado flesh
- 0.5 oz of agave syrup

Instructions

1. Combine all ingredients in a sizable bowl.
2. Fill a Ninja CREAMi Dessert Tub with the mixture.
3. Frozen for 24 hours with the lid on the tub.
4. Remove the cover off the tub and put it in the outer bowl after the 24-hour period has passed. Put the Creamerizer Paddle in place.
5. Lock the Outer Bowl into position on the motor base.
6. The machine can be started by pressing the power button.
7. then select smoothie bowl from the menu.
8. Release the outer bowl from the motor base once it has been finished. Take off the lid.
9. Serve and enjoy!

Nutrition:

- Kcal:174 Carbs:7g Fat:15g

- serves 2

Ingredients

- 8 oz of frozen mango pieces
- 8 oz plain yogurt
- 2 oz fresh orange juice
- 1 oz maple syrup
- 2.5 ml ground turmeric
- ⅛ teaspoon ground cinnamon
- ⅛ teaspoon ground ginger
- 1 pinch of ground black pepper

Instructions

1. Blend and pulse all ingredients in a high-speed blender until smooth.
2. Fill a Ninja CREAMi Dessert Tub with the mixture.
3. Frozen for 24 hours with the lid on the tub.
4. Remove the cover off the tub and put it in the outer bowl after the 24-hour period has passed. Put the Creamerizer Paddle in place.
5. Lock the Outer Bowl into position on the motor base.
6. The machine can be started by pressing the power button.
7. then select smoothie bowl from the menu.
8. Release the outer bowl from the motor base once it has been finished. Take off the lid.
9. Dispense and savor!

Nutrition:

- Kcal:179 Carbs:3g Fat:5g

- serves 2

Ingredients

- 8 oz canned pumpkin puree.
- 2 oz plain Greek yogurt
- 1½ tablespoons maple syrup
- 5 ml vanilla extract
- 5 ml pumpkin pie spice
- 1 frozen banana, cut into pieces.

Instructions

1. In a sizable bowl, combine the pumpkin puree, yogurt, maple syrup, vanilla essence, and pumpkin pie spice.
2. Stir in the banana chunks after adding them.
3. Fill a Ninja CREAMi Dessert Tub with the mixture.
4. Frozen for 24 hours with the lid on the tub.
5. Remove the cover off the tub and put it in the outer bowl after the 24-hour period has passed. Put the Creamerizer Paddle in place.
6. Lock the Outer Bowl into position on the motor base.
7. The machine can be started by pressing the power button.
8. then select smoothie bowl from the menu.
9. Release the outer bowl from the motor base once it has been finished. Take off the lid.
10. Dispense and savor!

Nutrition:

- Kcal:159 Carbs:9g Fat:10g Protein:6g

- serves 2

Ingredients

- 1 banana, cut into pieces
- ½ avocado cut into pieces
- 8 oz fresh kale leaves
- 8 oz green apple chopped
- 2 oz unsweetened coconut milk
- 1 oz agave syrup

Instructions

1. All the ingredients should be combined and blended in a high-speed blender just until the liquid is smooth.
2. Fill a Ninja CREAMi Dessert Tub with the mixture.
3. Frozen for 24 hours with the lid on the tub.
4. Remove the cover off the tub and put it in the outer bowl after the 24-hour period has passed. Put the Creamerizer Paddle in place.
5. Lock the Outer Bowl into position on the motor base.
6. The machine can be started by pressing the power button.
7. then select smoothie bowl from the menu.
8. Release the outer bowl from the motor base once it has been finished. Take off the lid.
9. Dispense and savor!

Nutrition:

- Kcal:140 Carbs:5g Fat:12g Protein:3g

- serves 2

Ingredients

- 2 oz instant coffee
- 8 oz unsweetened vanilla almond milk

Instructions

1. In a sizable mixing basin, stir the almond milk and instant coffee until fully blended and the coffee is dissolved.
2. Fill a Ninja CREAMi Dessert Tub with the mixture.
3. Frozen for 24 hours with the lid on the tub.
4. Remove the cover off the tub and put it in the outer bowl after the 24-hour period has passed. Put the Creamerizer Paddle in place.
5. Lock the Outer Bowl into position on the motor base.
6. The machine can be started by pressing the power button.
7. then select smoothie bowl from the menu.
8. Release the outer bowl from the motor base once it has been finished. Take off the lid.
9. Dispense and savor!

Nutrition:

- Kcal:270 Carbs:17g Fat:25g Protein:11g

- serves 2

Ingredients

- 1 banana, cut into pieces.
- 4 oz carrots, chopped
- 2 oz rolled oats
- 1 oz Greek yogurt with vanilla
- 2.5 ml ground cinnamon

Instructions

1. In a big bowl, combine banana, carrots, oatmeal, yogurt, and cinnamon.
2. Fill a Ninja CREAMi Dessert Tub with the mixture.
3. Frozen for 24 hours with the lid on the tub.
4. Remove the cover off the tub and put it in the outer bowl after the 24-hour period has passed. Put the Creamerizer Paddle in place.
5. Lock the Outer Bowl into position on the motor base.
6. The machine can be started by pressing the power button.
7. then select smoothie bowl from the menu.
8. Release the outer bowl from the motor base once it has been finished. Take off the lid.
9. Dispense and savor!

Nutrition:

- Kcal:370 Carbs:5g Fat:12g Protein:16g

Chapter 5:
- Lite ice cream recipes

48. Fruit Carrot Ice Cream

Ingredients

- 6 oz heavy cream
- 4 oz milk
- 2 oz orange juice
- 6 oz sugar
- 2 oz frozen carrots
- 2 oz pineapple chunks

Directions

1. In a bowl, whisk together the heavy cream, milk, orange juice, and sugar until the sugar is totally dissolved.
2. In an empty Ninja CREAMi pint container, layer the carrot and pineapple chunks with the milk mixture.
3. The container should be covered with a storage lid and frozen for 24 hours.
4. After 24 hours, take the cover off the jar and put it in the Ninja CREAMi Outer Bowl.
5. Place the Creamerizer Paddle on the outer bowl's lid.
6. To lock, turn the lid in a clockwise direction.
7. Turn the device on by pressing the Power button.
8. the Ice Cream button, then.

9. Turn the outer bowl and remove it from the machine after the program is finished.
10. If you want your processed treat to be softer and creamier after processing, select the Re-spin function.
11. Serve the ice cream right away after transferring it to serving bowls.

49. Chia Seed Ice Cream

Ingredients

- 2 oz milk
- 30 ml honey
- 4 oz vanilla whole milk Greek yogurt
- 30 ml chia seeds

Directions

1. The components should be combined and then smoothed out.
2. Pour the ingredients into a Ninja CREAMi Pint that is empty.
3. Place the pint in the freezer for 24 hours with the lid on.
4. Remove the lid after 24 hours and put the pint into the Ninja CREAMi's outer bowl.
5. Place the Creamerizer Paddle on the outer bowl's lid, then lock the lid by turning it clockwise.
6. Activate the device.
7. Activate the ICE CREAM button.
8. Turn the outer bowl and release it from the device once the program is finished.
9. If you want your processed treat to be softer and creamier after processing, select the Re-spin function.
10. Put food in bowls.

50. Vanilla Ice Cream

Ingredients

- 6 frozen bananas, peeled.
- 2 oz ultra-filtered 2% milk
- 1/2 cup Greek yogurt
- 15 ml honey
- 1.2 ml pure vanilla extract
- 1/2 teaspoon pink Himalayan salt, crushed.

Directions

1. In a sizable mixing bowl, combine all the ingredients.
2. Transfer to the pint container for Ninja Creami.
3. Blend until uniform.
4. If you want your processed treat to be softer and creamier after processing, select the Re-spin function.
5. Place leftovers in separate bowls before freezing them in an airtight container.

51. Bourbon Ice Cream

Ingredients

- 6 frozen bananas, peeled.
- 8 oz Greek yogurt
- 5 ml pure vanilla extract
- 2 oz brown sugar substitute
- 15 ml bourbon

Directions

1. To a big mixing bowl, add all the ingredients.
2. The Ninja Creami pint container should be transferred.
3. Blend thoroughly.
4. If you want your processed treat to be creamier and softer after processing, use the Re-spin option.
5. Remaining food should be divided among dishes before being frozen in an airtight container.

52.   Coconut Caramel Ice Cream

Ingredients

- 6 frozen bananas, peeled.
- 1 bag fresh frozen coconut
- 5 ml pure coconut extract
- 5 ml brown sugar substitute
- 2 teaspoons pure vanilla extract
- 2 oz calorie free caramel sauce

Directions

1. In a sizable mixing bowl, combine all the ingredients.
2. Transfer to the pint container for Ninja Creami.
3. Blend until uniform.
4. If you want your processed treat to be softer and creamier after processing, select the Re-spin function.
5. Place leftovers in separate bowls before freezing them in an airtight container.
6. Add caramel sauce on top.
7. Leftovers should be frozen in an airtight container.

53.   Mint Chocolate Chip Ice Cream

Ingredients

- 9 frozen bananas, peeled.
- 1/2 frozen avocado, peeled and pitted
- 15 ml honey
- 5 mint leaves, chopped.
- 1/2 teaspoon mint extract
- 3 oz 85% dark cacao bar, chopped.

Directions

1. In a sizable mixing bowl, combine all the ingredients.
2. Transfer to the pint container for Ninja Creami.
3. Blend until uniform.
4. If you want your processed treat to be softer and creamier after processing, select the Re-spin function.
5. Place leftovers in separate bowls before freezing them in an airtight container.

54. Peanut Butter Pretzel Ice Cream

Ingredients

- 12 frozen bananas, peeled.
- 15 ml all-natural peanut butter, no sugar added.
- 5 ml honey
- 1.2 ml pure vanilla extract, frozen
- 15 ml ultra-filtered milk or almond milk, frozen
- 1/2 cup gluten-free pretzels roughly chopped.

Directions

1. In a sizable mixing basin, combine the milk, butter, honey, vanilla essence, and bananas.
2. Transfer to the pint container for Ninja Creami.
3. Blend until uniform.
4. If you want your processed treat to be softer and creamier after processing, select the Re-spin function.
5. Place ice cream in waffle cones, then sprinkle pretzel bits on top.
6. In an airtight container, freeze any remaining soft serve..

55. Chocolate Ice Cream

Ingredients

- 12 frozen bananas, peeled.
- 8 oz Greek yogurt, vanilla flavored
- 1/2 cup unsweetened cocoa
- 1/2 cup coffee
- 15 ml Neufchatel or cream cheese substitute
- 30 ml honey
- 3 oz bittersweet chocolate chips
- 3 oz peanut butter chips

Directions

1. Place the coffee, Greek yogurt, and unsweetened chocolate in a sizable mixing dish.
2. Whip it up until soft peaks emerge. Place in the fridge for two hours to chill.
3. To a sizable mixing bowl, add the remaining ingredients.
4. Transfer to the pint container for Ninja Creami.
5. Blend until uniform.
6. If you want your processed treat to be softer and creamier after processing, select the Re-spin function.
7. Place leftovers in separate bowls before freezing them in an airtight container.

56. Sugar-free Coconut Vanilla Ice Cream

Ingredients

- 6 frozen bananas, peeled.
- 15 ml unsweetened coconut milk
- 5 ml pure vanilla extract
- 1/2 teaspoon pure coconut extract
- 1/2 teaspoon sugar substitute (like Stevia)

Directions

1. In a sizable mixing bowl, combine all the ingredients.
2. Transfer to the pint container for Ninja Creami.
3. Blend until uniform.
4. If you want your processed treat to be softer and creamier after processing, select the Re-spin function.
5. Place leftovers in separate bowls before freezing them in an airtight container.

57. Chocolate Peanut Butter Banana Ice Cream

Ingredients

- 9 frozen bananas, peeled.
- 30 ml natural peanut butter, no sugar added.
- 3 oz 85% dark cacao bar, chopped.

Directions

1. In a sizable mixing bowl, combine all the ingredients.
2. Transfer to the pint container for Ninja Creami.
3. Blend until uniform.
4. If you want your processed treat to be softer and creamier after processing, select the Re-spin function.
5. Divvy up into individual bowls and sprinkle with chunks of dark chocolate.
6. Leftovers should be frozen in an airtight container.

58. Strawberry Banana Ice Cream

Ingredients

- 8 frozen bananas, peeled.
- 8 oz frozen strawberries

Directions

1. In a sizable mixing bowl, combine all the ingredients.
2. Transfer to the pint container for Ninja Creami.
3. Blend until uniform.
4. If you want your processed treat to be softer and creamier after processing, select the Re-spin function.
5. Place leftovers in separate bowls before freezing them in an airtight container.

59. Vanilla Avocado Banana Ice Cream

Ingredients

- 9 frozen bananas, peeled.
- 1 frozen avocado peeled and pitted.
- 15 ml honey
- 5 ml pure vanilla extract

Directions

1. To a sizable mixing basin, add each ingredient.
2. Transfer to the pint-sized Ninja Creami container.
3. Mix thoroughly.
4. If after processing you want your treat to be softer and creamier, choose the Re-spin mode.
5. Put leftovers in individual bowls and freeze them in a freezer-safe container.

Chapter 6:
- Milkshakes recipes

60. Almond & Candy Bar Milkshake

- Servings: 2
- Preparation Time: 5 minutes
- Freeze Time: 0 hours.

Ingredients:

- 1 4 ozs coco leche ice cream
- 4 oz almond milk
- 1 oz chocolate chips
- 1 oz almonds roasted and chopped.

Method:

- Add all the ingredients to the Ninja Creami pint container.
- Place the container in the machine.
- Select the Milkshake setting.

Nutrition:

- Energy - 188 kcal
- Fat - 14.9 g
- Carbs - 5.0 g

Ingredients

- 14 ozs Dark Chocolate Ice Cream
- 4 oz unsweetened chocolate almond milk

Instructions

1. In a Ninja CREAMi Dessert Tub, place the chocolate ice cream and almond milk.
2. Place the tub in the Outer Bowl. Install the Creamerizer Paddle.
3. Place the Outer Bowl on the motor base and lock it.
4. Turn ON the NINJA CREAMi and press the MILKSHAKE button.
5. Once the program is finished, release the Outer Bowl from the motor base and remove the lid.
6. Serve the milkshake with the topping of your choice, and enjoy!

Nutrition:

- Energy - 196 kcal
- Fat - 13.0 g
- Carbs - 6.9 g

Ingredients

- 14 ozs Vanilla Ice Cream
- 2 oz peanut butter
- 2 oz Mini Oreo cookies

Instructions

1. Place the vanilla ice cream in a Ninja CREAMi Dessert Tub and scoop a hole in the middle that goes to the bottom.
2. Put the peanut butter and Oreo in the hole that you created.
3. Place the tub in the Outer Bowl. Install the Creamerizer Paddle.
4. Place the Outer Bowl on the motor base and lock it.
5. Turn ON the NINJA CREAMi and press the MILKSHAKE button.
6. Once the program is finished, release the Outer Bowl from the motor base and remove the lid.
7. Serve the milkshake with the topping of your choice, and enjoy!

Nutrition:

- Energy - 300 kcal
- Fat - 23.9 g

Ingredients

- 8 oz Vanilla Ice Cream
- 2 oz unsweetened almond milk
- 2 tsp unsweetened cocoa powder
- ¼ tsp peppermint extract
- ¼ tsp dried mint leaves

Instructions

1. Place all ingredients in a Ninja CREAMi Dessert Tub.
2. Place the tub in the Outer Bowl. Install the Creamerizer Paddle.
3. Place the Outer Bowl on the motor base and lock it.
4. Turn ON the NINJA CREAMi and press the MILKSHAKE button.
5. Once the program is finished, release the Outer Bowl from the motor base and remove the lid.
6. Serve the milkshake with the topping of your choice, and enjoy!

Nutrition:

- Energy - 170 kcal
- Fat - 13.0 g

Ingredients

- 8 oz Vanilla Ice Cream
- 2 oz unsweetened almond milk
- 1 tsp vanilla extract
- ¼ tsp ground cinnamon
- ¼ tsp ground nutmeg
- Pinch of sea salt

Instructions

1. Place all ingredients in a Ninja CREAMi Dessert Tub.
2. Place the tub in the Outer Bowl. Install the Creamerizer Paddle.
3. Place the Outer Bowl on the motor base and lock it.
4. Turn ON the NINJA CREAMi and press the MILKSHAKE button.
5. Once the program is finished, release the Outer Bowl from the motor base and remove the lid.
6. Serve the milkshake with the topping of your choice and enjoy!

Nutrition:

- Energy - 120 kcal
- Fat - 33.9 g

65. Peanut Butter Shake

Ingredients

- 2 oz heavy cream
- 2 oz strawberries
- 3 tbsp natural peanut butter
- 4 oz unsweetened almond milk
- 1 tsp pure vanilla extract

Instructions

1. Place all ingredients in a Ninja CREAMi Dessert Tub.
2. Place the tub in the Outer Bowl. Install the Creamerizer Paddle.
3. Place the Outer Bowl on the motor base and lock it.
4. Turn ON the NINJA CREAMi and press the MILKSHAKE button.
5. Once the program is finished, release the Outer Bowl from the motor base and remove the lid.
6. Serve the milkshake with the topping of your choice, and enjoy!

Nutrition:

- Energy - 186 kcal
- Fat - 13.9 g
- Carbs - 5.9 g

66. Mocha Shake

Ingredients

- 4 oz unsweetened almond milk
- 2 oz heavy cream
- 1½ tbsp MTC oil
- 2 tbsp instant coffee
- 1½ tbsp cocoa powder

Instructions

1. Place all ingredients in a Ninja CREAMi Dessert Tub.
2. Place the tub in the Outer Bowl. Install the Creamerizer Paddle.
3. Place the Outer Bowl on the motor base and lock it.
4. Turn ON the NINJA CREAMi and press the MILKSHAKE button.
5. Once the program is finished, release the Outer Bowl from the motor base and remove the lid.
6. Serve the milkshake with the topping of your choice, and enjoy!

Nutrition:

- Energy - 286 kcal
- Carbs - 45.9 g
- Protein - 20.6 g

Ingredients

- 2 oz blueberries
- ⅔ cup unsweetened almond milk
- 1 scoop vanilla protein powder
- 2 tbsp natural almond butter
- ¼ tsp ground cinnamon

Instructions

1. Place all ingredients in a Ninja CREAMi Dessert Tub.
2. Place the tub in the Outer Bowl. Install the Creamerizer Paddle.
3. Place the Outer Bowl on the motor base and lock it.
4. Turn ON the NINJA CREAMi and press the MILKSHAKE button.
5. Once the program is finished, release the Outer Bowl from the motor base and remove the lid.
6. Serve the milkshake with the topping of your choice and enjoy!

Nutrition:

- Energy - 200 kcal
- Fat - 43.9 g

68. Raspberry-Chocolate Shake

Ingredients

- 2 oz heavy cream
- 2 oz raspberries
- 1 scoop of chocolate protein powder
- 1 tbsp cocoa powder
- 4 oz unsweetened almond milk

Instructions

1. Place all ingredients in a Ninja CREAMi Dessert Tub.
2. Place the tub in the Outer Bowl. Install the Creamerizer Paddle.
3. Place the Outer Bowl on the motor base and lock it.
4. Turn ON the NINJA CREAMi and press the MILKSHAKE button.
5. Once the program is finished, release the Outer Bowl from the motor base and remove the lid.
6. Serve the milkshake with the topping of your choice, and enjoy!

Nutrition:

- Energy - 201 kcal
- Fat - 23.9 g
- Carbs - 12.9 g

- Prep time: 5 minutes
- Cook time: 10 minutes
- Serves 1

Ingredients:

- 8 oz milk
- 0.5 oz honey
- 2.5 ml vanilla extract
- 4 oz frozen strawberries

Directions:

1. Fill an empty CREAMi Pint with milk, honey, vanilla essence, and strawberries. Install the Creamerizer Paddle onto the outer bowl lid and secure the lid assembly to the outer bowl. Position the bowl assembly on the motor base and crank the lever to raise and secure the platform. Choose MILKSHAKE.
2. After the processing is complete, remove the milkshake from the pint

Nutrition:

- Kcal: 29 Protein: 0.7 Fat: 0.3 Carbs: 7.8.

- Prep time: 5 minutes
- Cook time: 5 minutes
- Serves 2

Ingredients:

- 8 oz coconut ice cream
- 1 small ripe avocado, peeled, pitted, and chopped
- 5 ml fresh lemon juice
- 1 oz agave nectar
- 5 ml vanilla extract
- Pinch of salt
- 4 oz oat milk

Directions:

1. Put the ice cream and the rest of the ingredients in an empty Ninja CREAMi pint container.
   Arrange the container in the Ninja CREAMi outer bowl.
   Attach the "Creamerizer Paddle" to the outer bowl's cover.
2. Then, to lock it, twist the lid clockwise.
3. To turn on the machine, press the "Power" button.
4. Then click the "MILKSHAKE" button.
5. When the program is finished, remove the outer bowl from the machine.
6. Pour the shake into serving glasses and serve right away

Nutrition:

- Fat - 9.1 g
- Carbs - 16.0 g Protein - 9.7 g.

71. Chocolate Cherry Milkshake

- Prep time: 5 minutes
- Cook time: 4 minutes.
- Serves 4

Ingredients:

- 14 ozs chocolate ice cream
- 4 oz canned cherries in syrup, drained
- 2 oz whole milk

Directions:

1. Place the ice cream, cherries, and milk in an empty Ninja CREAMi pint container. 2. Place the container in the Ninja CREAMi Outer Bowl.
   Place the Creamerizer Paddle on the lid of the Outer Bowl.
   Then, to lock it, twist the lid clockwise.
2. To turn on the device, press the power button.
3. Then click the Milkshake button.
4. When the program is finished, remove the outer bowl from the machine.
5. Pour the shake into serving glasses and serve right away.

Nutrition

- Kcal 291, fat 8 g, carbs 53 g, sugar 50 g

72. Lemon Meringue Pie Milkshake

- Prep time: 5 minutes
- Cook time: 5 minutes.
- Serves 1

Ingredients:

- 8 oz vanilla ice cream
- 4 tablespoons store-bought lemon curd, divided
- 4 tablespoons marshmallow topping, divided
- 4 oz Graham Crackers, broken, divided

Directions:

1. Fill an empty CREAMi Pint with ice cream. Use a spoon to create a 112-inch wide hole in the bottom of the pint. Place the Creamerizer Paddle on the outer bowl lid and secure it to the outer bowl. Position the bowl assembly on the motor base and crank the lever to raise and secure the platform.
2. Choose the MILKSHAKE option.
3. After the processing is complete, remove the milkshake from the pint.

Nutrition:

- Energy - 198 kcal
- Fat - 10.1 g
- Carbs - 17.0 g
- Protein - 10.7 g Sodium - 252 mg

- Prep time: 5 minutes
- Cook time: 3 minutes.
- Serves 2

Ingredients:

- 8 oz vanilla ice cream
- 1 oz coffee liqueur
- 1 oz vodka

Directions:

1. Pour the ice cream, coffee liqueur, and vodka into an empty Ninja CREAMi pint container.
   Arrange the container in the Ninja CREAMi outer bowl. Attach the "Creamerizer Paddle" to the outer bowl's cover.
2. Then, to lock it, twist the lid clockwise.
3. To turn on the machine, press the "Power" button.
4. Then click the "MILKSHAKE" button.
5. When the program is finished, remove the outer bowl from the machine.
6. Pour the shake into serving glasses and serve right away.

Nutrition:

- Kcal: 900 Fat: 58.9g Carbs: 74.0g

74. Chocolate-hazelnut Milkshake

- Prep time: 5 minutes
- Cook time: 3 minutes.
- Serves 4

Ingredients:

- 1 oz granulated sugar
- 1 oz unsweetened cocoa powder
- 4 oz whole milk
- 8 oz hazelnut-flavored coffee creamer

Directions:

1. Whisk the sugar, cocoa powder, milk, and coffee creamer in a large mixing basin until the sugar is completely dissolved.
   Pour the base into a clean CREAMi Pint. Freeze the container for 24 hours with the storage cover on.
   Take the pint out of the freezer and remove the lid. Install the Creamerizer Paddle in your Ninja CREAMi's outer bowl lid, then lock the lid assembly onto the outside bowl. Place the bowl assembly on the motor base and twist the handle to the right to elevate and secure the platform. Choose the Milkshake option.
2. Remove the milkshake from the pint after the machine has done processing. Serve immediately.

Nutrition:

- Fat - 10.1 g
- Carbs - 17.0 g
- Protein - 10.7 g

Chapter 7:
- Sorbets recipes

75. Orange Sorbet

- serves 2

Ingredients

- 8 oz orange juice
- 2 teaspoons star anise
- 4 oz sugar

Instructions

1. In a high-speed blender, combine all the ingredients and blend just until the mixture is smooth.
2. Fill a Ninja CREAMi Dessert Tub with the mixture.
3. Frozen for 24 hours with the lid on the tub.
4. Remove the cover off the tub and put it in the outer bowl after the 24-hour period has passed. Put the Creamerizer Paddle in place.
5. Lock the Outer Bowl into position on the motor base.
6. The machine can be started by pressing the power button.
7. Sorbet button should then be pressed.
8. Release the outer bowl from the motor base once it has been finished. Take off the lid.

9. Offer and savor!

Nutrition:

- Kcal:110 Carbs:1g Fat:9g Protein:2g

- serves 2

Ingredients

- 8 oz of blueberries
- 8 oz raspberries
- 8 oz strawberries chopped.

Instructions

1. Using a potato masher, mash the berries in a Ninja CREAMi Dessert Tub until well-combined.
2. Frozen for 24 hours with the lid on the tub.
3. Remove the cover off the tub and put it in the outer bowl after the 24-hour period has passed. Put the Creamerizer Paddle in place.
4. Lock the Outer Bowl into position on the motor base.
5. The machine can be started by pressing the power button.
6. Sorbet button should then be pressed.
7. Release the outer bowl from the motor base once it has been finished. Take off the lid.
8. Offer and savor!

Nutrition:

- Kcal:180 Carbs:9g Fat:25g Protein:5g

77. Grape Sorbet

- Serves 2

Ingredients

- 6 oz concentrated grape juice
- 14 ozs water
- 0.5 oz fresh lemon juice

Instructions

1. Place all ingredients in a bowl and stir to thoroughly blend.
2. Fill a Ninja CREAMi Dessert Tub with the mixture.
3. Frozen for 24 hours with the lid on the tub.
4. Remove the cover off the tub and put it in the outer bowl after the 24-hour period has passed. Put the Creamerizer Paddle in place.
5. Lock the Outer Bowl into position on the motor base.
6. The machine can be started by pressing the power button.
7. Sorbet button should then be pressed.
8. Release the outer bowl from the motor base once it has been finished. Take off the lid.

Nutrition:

- Kcal:130 Carbs:3g Fat:10g Protein:2g

- Serves 2

Ingredients

- 8 oz sliced strawberries
- 4 kiwis chopped
- 2 oz agave syrup
- 2 oz water

Instructions

1. In a high-speed blender, combine all the ingredients and blend just until the mixture is smooth.
2. Fill a Ninja CREAMi Dessert Tub with the mixture.
3. Frozen for 24 hours with the lid on the tub.
4. Remove the cover off the tub and put it in the outer bowl after the 24-hour period has passed. Put the Creamerizer Paddle in place.
5. Lock the Outer Bowl into position on the motor base.
6. The machine can be started by pressing the power button.
7. Press the Sorbet button after that.
8. Release the outer bowl from the motor base once it has been finished. Take off the lid.

Nutrition:

- Kcal:140 Carbs:9g Fat:11g Protein:11g

- Serves 2

Ingredients

- 4 oz water
- 4 oz white sugar
- 2 oz mint leaves
- 5 ml grated lime zest
- 4 oz freshly squeezed lime juice
- 6 oz citrus-flavored sparkling water

Instructions

1. Place all ingredients in a bowl and mix until sugar is dissolved.
2. Transfer the mixture to a Ninja CREAMi Dessert Tub.
3. Cover the tub with a lid and freeze for 24 hours.
4. After 24 hours, remove the lid from the tub and place it in the Outer Bowl. Install the Creamerizer Paddle.
5. Place the Outer Bowl on the motor base and lock it in place.

Nutrition:

- Kcal:160 Carbs:9g Fat:35g Protein:12g

- Serves 4

Ingredients

- 16 oz canned pineapple pieces with juice
- 5 ml lemon juice
- 5 ml lemon zest
- 1 small piece of sliced ginger
- 5 ml basil leaves
- 2 oz white powdered sugar

Instructions

1. Put all the ingredients and pulse in a high-speed blender until the mixture is smooth.
2. Transfer the mixture to a Ninja CREAMi Dessert Tub.
3. Cover the tub with a lid and freeze for 24 hours.
4. After 24 hours, remove the lid from the tub and place it in the Outer Bowl. Install the Creamerizer Paddle.
5. Place the Outer Bowl on the motor base and lock it in place.
6. Press the power button to turn the machine on.

Nutrition:

- Kcal:270 Carbs:6g Fat: 09g Protein:10g

- Serves 2

Ingredients

- 4 cups chopped mango.
- 4 oz water
- 2 oz sugar
- 2 oz fresh lime juice

Instructions

1. Place the mango and water in a high-speed blender and pulse until smooth.
2. Strain the mango puree through a fine-mesh sieve into a large bowl.
3. Add sugar and lime juice and mix well.
4. Transfer the mixture to a Ninja CREAMi Dessert Tub.
5. Cover the tub with a lid and freeze for 24 hours.
6. After 24 hours, remove the lid from the tub and place it in the Outer Bowl. Install the Creamerizer Paddle.
7. Place the Outer Bowl on the motor base and lock it in place.
8. Press the power button to turn the machine on.

Nutrition:

- Kcal:145 Carbs:9g Fat:13g Protein:2g

- Serves 2

Ingredients

- 1 packet frozen açaí
- 4 oz blackberries
- 4 oz banana, sliced
- 2 oz granulated sugar
- 8 oz water

Instructions

1. Put all the ingredients and pulse in a high-speed blender until the mixture is smooth.
2. Transfer the mixture to a Ninja CREAMi Dessert Tub.
3. Cover the tub with a lid and freeze for 24 hours.
4. After 24 hours, remove the lid from the tub and place it in the Outer Bowl. Install the Creamerizer Paddle.
5. Place the Outer Bowl on the motor base and lock it in place.
6. Press the power button to turn the machine on.

Nutrition:

- Kcal:180 Carbs:7g Fat:15g Protein:1g

83. Watermelon Sorbet

- Serves 2

Ingredients

- 34 ozs seedless watermelon pieces.
- 2 teaspoons lime juice
- 2 oz water

Instructions

1. In a high-speed blender, add all ingredients and blend until smooth.
2. Transfer the mixture to a Ninja CREAMi Dessert Tub.
3. Cover the tub with a lid and freeze for 24 hours.
4. After 24 hours, remove the lid from the tub and place it in the Outer Bowl. Install the Creamerizer Paddle.
5. Place the Outer Bowl on the motor base and lock it in place.
6. Press the power button to turn the machine on.

Nutrition:

- Kcal:123 Carbs:7g Fat:19g Protein:3g

- Serves 2

Ingredients

- 2 large bananas cut into pieces.
- Water, if necessary

Instructions

1. In a blender on high speed, add the bananas and a little water and blend until the mixture is smooth.
2. Transfer the mixture to a Ninja CREAMi Dessert Tub.
3. Cover the tub with a lid and freeze for 24 hours.
4. After 24 hours, remove the lid from the tub and place it in the Outer Bowl. Install the Creamerizer Paddle.
5. Place the Outer Bowl on the motor base and lock it in place.
6. Press the power button to turn the machine on.

Nutrition:

- Kcal:190 Carbs:7g Fat:13g Protein:4g

- Preparation
- Total Time: 10 minutes

Ingredients:

- 2 bananas sliced and frozen.
- 8 oz frozen mango
- 8 oz frozen pineapple

Directions:

1. Run half the bananas through your Healthy Dessert Maker.
2. Press down on the plunger.
3. Repeat steps 1 and 2 with the mango, pineapple, and remaining bananas.
4. Stir to mix the flavors.

Nutrition:

- Kcal: 26 Protein: 0.07 Fat: 0.03 Carbs: 6.8

- Preparation
- Total Time: 30 minutes

Ingredients:

- 8 cups frozen papaya
- 2 Tbsp. lime juice
- 2 pinches of salt
- 1 tsp lime zest
- 4 oz water
- 4 oz sugar
- 2 oz coconut milk, canned and chilled

Directions:

1. Over medium to high heat, bring water and sugar to a boil until the sugar is completely dissolved (about 3-5 minutes).
2. To avoid burning, make sure to stir often. reserve for cooling.
3. Add one-fourth of the papayas, one-fourth of the syrup, 0.5 ounces of milk, one-half tablespoon of lime juice, one-fourth teaspoon of zest, and a dash of salt.
4. The plunger must be depressed.
5. Repeat steps 2 and 3 a total of four more times to use all the ingredients.

Nutrition:

- Kcal: 28 Protein: 0.8 Fat: 0.3 Carbs: 7.8

87. Fresh and Fruity Pineapple-Coconut Sorbet

- Preparation
- Total Time:25 minutes

Ingredients:

- 3 ¼ in. thick ginger, peeled and crushed
- 2 tsp lime juice
- 1 pineapple, chopped and frozen
- 4 oz sugar
- 4 oz coconut milk, canned and chilled

Directions:

1. Simmer coconut milk, sugar, and ginger over medium heat. Bring to a boil. Set aside.
2. Pour the mixture into a bowl after it has cooled, then reserve.
3. Run ½ the pineapple mixture, ½ the coconut mixture, and ½ the lime juice
4. Press down on the plunger.
5. Repeat steps 3 and 4.

Nutrition:

- Kcal: 28 Protein: 0.09 Fat: 0.07 Carbs: 5.7

- Preparation
- Total Time:2 hours 45 minutes

Ingredients:

- 4 Earl Grey tea bags
- 4 cups water
- 8 oz unsweetened cocoa powder
- 1 oz. bitter chocolate, chopped.
- 6 oz sugar

Directions:

1. Sugar and water are brought to a boil.
2. After adding the tea bags to the water and sugar combination, turn off the heat. Take 15 minutes to move.
3. Throw away the tea bags and put the mixture back over medium-high heat.
4. Blend in the cocoa powder after adding it.
5. Simmer for 20 minutes on low heat.
6. Once the chocolate is completely melted, remove from the fire.
7. After two hours of freezing, strain the mixture.
8. Cut into pieces and feed.

Nutrition

- Kcal: 30 Protein: 0.03 Fat: 0.06 Carbs: 6.6

Chapter 8:
- Gelato recipes

89. Lemon Gelato

Ingredients

- 8 oz whole milk
- 8 oz granulated sugar
- 15 ml grated lemon zest
- 6 oz lemon juice
- 8 oz heavy cream

Directions

1. According to the manufacturer's recommendations, freeze the ice cream machine bowl for 12 to 24 hours.
2. In the meantime, heat the whole milk, sugar, and lemon zest in a saucepan over medium heat. Stir the sugar until it completely dissolves. For around 10 to 12 minutes, bring the mixture to a gentle simmer.
3. Pour into a tidy bowl—ideally one with a spout—and place aside. Add heavy cream and lemon juice after stirring. Assemble by combining.
4. At room temperature, allow the mixture to cool.
5. The mixture should cool in the refrigerator for at least 2 to 12 hours after being covered with plastic wrap.

6. Take the gelato mixture out of the fridge and give it a couple stirs.
7. After installing it, pour the gelato mixture into the ice cream maker bowl.
8. While the machine is connected, press the start and gelato buttons.
9. After the cycle is finished, either serve the gelato right away or transfer it to an airtight, freezer-safe container. It'll be a smooth, creamy gelato. If you like a firmer texture, freeze the gelato for at least two hours prior to serving.

Prep

*   Kcal 341, fat 14 g, carbs 56 g

90. Biscotti Gelato

Ingredients

- Eight oz whole milk
- 8 oz heavy cream
- 6 oz granulated sugar
- 30 ml honey
- 5 ml almond extract
- 4 oz crushed biscotti cookies

Directions

1. Freeze the ice cream maker bowl for 12 to 24 hours in accordance with the manufacturer's instructions.
2. Meanwhile, warm the whole milk, honey, and granulated sugar in a medium saucepan over medium heat until the honey and sugar have completely dissolved.
3. After turning off the heat, add the heavy cream and almond essence by stirring. Put together through merging.
4. Pouring the mixture into a clean basin with a spout will allow it to cool naturally.
5. The mixture should cool in the refrigerator for at least 2 to 12 hours after being covered with plastic wrap.
6. Take the gelato mixture out of the fridge and give it a couple stirs.
7. Pour the gelato mixture into the bowl of the ice cream machine.
8. Press the start and gelato buttons while the machine is connected.
9. Add the smashed biscotti cookies to the gelato gradually as it is being churned, around 5 minutes before it is finished.
10. After the cycle is complete, either serve the gelato immediately away or move it to a freezer-safe, airtight container. It will be a creamy, silky gelato. Before serving, let the gelato freeze for at least two hours if you prefer a firmer texture.

Prep

- Kcal 412, fat 17 g, carbs 64 g

91. Panna Cotta Gelato

Ingredients

- 8 oz whole milk
- 8 oz heavy cream
- ⅔ cup granulated sugar
- 5 ml vanilla extract

Directions

1. Freeze the ice cream maker bowl for 12 to 24 hours in accordance with the manufacturer's instructions.
2. Cook the whole milk, heavy cream, and granulated sugar in a medium saucepan for 10 to 12 minutes on medium heat while this is going on.
3. The sugar must be completely cooked for it to dissolve. Stir the mixture often up until it thickens. The best indicator of fistedness is when the mixture coats the back of a spoon.
4. After removing the pan from the heat, whisk in the vanilla essence. Put together through merging.
5. The entire mixture should be poured into a clean bowl with a spout and allowed to cool to room temperature.
6. After being wrapped in plastic wrap, the mixture should cool in the refrigerator for at least 2 to 12 hours.
7. Remove the gelato mixture from the refrigerator and whisk it a few times.
8. After installing it, pour the gelato mixture into the ice cream maker bowl.
9. While the machine is connected, press the start and gelato buttons.
10. After the cycle is finished, either serve the gelato right away or transfer it to an airtight, freezer-safe container. It'll be a smooth, creamy gelato. If you like a firmer texture, freeze the gelato for at least two hours prior to serving.

Prep

- Kcal 314, fat 16 g, carbs 41 g

Ingredients

- Eight oz whole milk
- 8 oz heavy cream
- 6 oz granulated sugar
- Five ml vanilla extract
- 6 tablespoons pistachio paste

Directions

1. Freeze the ice cream maker bowl for 12 to 24 hours as directed by the manufacturer.
2. Reheat the heavy cream, sugar, and whole milk in a medium saucepan over low heat in the interim.
3. To dissolve all the sugar, simmer. For 15 to 20 minutes, whisk continuously until the mixture thickens. The best indicator of when the mixture is done is when it coats the back of a spoon.
4. Add the vanilla extract and pistachio paste after removing from the heat. Blend thoroughly and thoroughly. Transfer to a fresh bowl, ideally one that has a spout.
5. For at least two hours up to twelve hours, cover with plastic wrap and place in the refrigerator.
6. Take the gelato mixture out of the fridge and give it a couple stirs.
7. Pour the ingredients into the ice cream machine after setting up the bowl. Press the start and gelato buttons while the machine is connected.
8. After the cycle is complete, either serve the gelato immediately away or move it to a freezer-safe, airtight container. It will be a creamy, silky gelato. Before serving, let the gelato freeze for at least two hours if you prefer a firmer texture.

Prep

- Kcal 448, fat 25 g, carbs 53 g

93. Strawberry Gelato

Ingredients

- Eight oz whole milk
- 4 oz heavy cream
- 6 oz icing sugar
- 15 ml light corn syrup
- Five ml vanilla extract
- 5 ml lemon juice
- 2 4 oz chopped strawberries.

Directions

1. Freeze the ice cream maker bowl for 12 to 24 hours in accordance with the manufacturer's instructions.
2. Then, in a high-speed blender or food processor, combine the whole milk, heavy cream, icing sugar, light corn syrup, vanilla extract, lemon juice, and strawberry slices.
3. After everything has been combined, blitz until a smooth mixture forms.
4. In a brand-new bowl with a spout, place the gelato base, and stir to incorporate.
5. After being wrapped in plastic wrap, the mixture should cool in the refrigerator for at least 2 to 12 hours.
6. Take the gelato mixture out of the fridge and give it a couple stirs.
7. Fill the ice cream maker's bowl with the gelato mixture.
8. Press the start and gelato buttons while the machine is connected.
9. After the cycle is complete, either serve the gelato immediately away or move it to a freezer-safe, airtight container. It will be a creamy, silky gelato. Before serving, let the gelato freeze for at least two hours if you prefer a firmer texture.

Prep

- Kcal 285, fat 10 g, carbs 46 g

Ingredients

- 7 oz whole milk
- Eight oz heavy cream
- 2/3 cup granulated sugar.
- Five ml vanilla extract
- 5 ml hazelnut extract
- 6 tablespoons hazelnut butter

Directions

1. Freeze the ice cream maker bowl for 12 to 24 hours in accordance with the manufacturer's instructions.
2. Reheat the whole milk and sugar granules in a medium saucepan over medium heat in the interim.
3. Stirring occasionally, simmer for 15 to 20 minutes, or until it almost reaches boiling, until the whole sugar is dissolved.
4. After removing from the heat, mix in the vanilla extract, hazelnut butter, and hazelnut essence. Before adding the heavy cream, thoroughly and evenly combine.
5. After being allowed to cool to room temperature, the entire liquid should be poured into a spotless bowl with a spout.
6. After being wrapped in plastic wrap, the mixture should cool in the refrigerator for at least 2 to 12 hours.
7. Remove the gelato mixture from the refrigerator and whisk it a few times.
8. After installing it, pour the gelato mixture into the ice cream maker bowl.
9. Press the start and gelato buttons while the machine is connected.
10. After the cycle is complete, either serve the gelato immediately away or move it to a freezer-safe, airtight container. It will be a creamy, silky gelato. Before serving, let the gelato freeze for at least two hours if you prefer a firmer texture.

Prep

- Kcal 477, fat 32 g, carbs 41 g

Ingredients

- 2 4 oz whole milk
- 8 oz heavy cream
- 2 pound very ripe mango diced into cubes.
- 2/3 cup icing sugar
- 5 ml vanilla extract

Directions

1. Freeze the ice cream maker bowl for 12 to 24 hours in accordance with the manufacturer's instructions.
2. In the meantime, puree the milk, mango cubes, and icing sugar in a powerful blender.
3. Blend till creamy and smooth. To get an even blend and a smoother texture for the gelato foundation, work in two or three batches if your blender is smaller.
4. After transferring the mango puree to a clean bowl, preferably one with a spout, add the heavy cream and vanilla extract.
5. After being wrapped in plastic wrap, the mixture should cool in the refrigerator for at least 2 to 12 hours.
6. Take the gelato mixture out of the fridge and give it a couple stirs.
7. Place the gelato mixture in the ice cream maker bowl.
8. Press the start and gelato buttons while the machine is connected.
9. After the cycle is complete, either serve the gelato immediately away or move it to a freezer-safe, airtight container. It will be a creamy, silky gelato. Before serving, let the gelato freeze for at least two hours if you prefer a firmer texture.

Prep

- Kcal 412, fat 17 g, carbs 62 g

Ingredients

- 2 4 oz whole milk
- 7 egg yolks
- 4 oz heavy cream
- 8 oz granulated sugar
- 15 ml vanilla extract

Directions

1. According to the manufacturer's recommendations, freeze the ice cream machine bowl for 12 to 24 hours.
2. In the meantime, cook the heavy cream, sugar, and milk in a saucepan over medium heat. For around 15 to 20 minutes, boil the mixture gently. Place aside.
3. Pour the hot milk mixture over the whisked egg yolks in another bowl. So that the eggs don't turn into scrambled eggs, whisk continually.
4. Add the vanilla and mix.
5. Re-heat the entire mixture over medium heat, stirring occasionally, until it has a smooth and creamy consistency. Pour the mixture back into the saucepan.
6. Make sure there are no small egg yolk particles in the gelato foundation by straining it through a fine-mesh sieve into a clean basin, preferably one with a spout.
7. The mixture should cool in the refrigerator for at least 2 to 12 hours after being covered with plastic wrap.
8. Take the gelato mixture out of the fridge and give it a couple stirs.
9. Pour the gelato mixture into the bowl of the frozen ice cream machine.
10. Press the start and gelato buttons while the machine is connected.
11. After the cycle is complete, either serve the gelato immediately away or move it to a freezer-safe, airtight container. It will be a creamy, silky gelato. Before serving, let the gelato freeze for at least two hours if you prefer a firmer texture.

Prep

- Kcal 434, fat 18 g, carbs 59 g

Ingredients

- 24 oz whole milk
- 5 oz. bittersweet chocolate, chopped into smaller pieces.
- 2 oz cocoa powder
- 8 oz granulated sugar.
- 30 ml instant chocolate pudding

Directions

1. Freeze the ice cream maker bowl for 12 to 24 hours in accordance with the manufacturer's instructions.
2. In the interim, warm 8 ounces of the whole milk in a saucepan over low heat.
3. Turn off the heat after allowing the mixture to simmer gently for 15 to 20 minutes. Mix well before adding the chopped bittersweet chocolate. Let it melt all the way.
4. In a separate pan, heat 8 ounces of whole milk over low heat while incorporating sugar, cocoa powder, and instant chocolate pudding.
5. Then, combine the two mixtures, reheat everything, and simmer everything for a further few minutes until it thickens.
6. Put the gelato base in a clean bowl, preferably one with a spout, after removing it from the heat.
7. After being wrapped in plastic wrap, the mixture should cool in the refrigerator for at least 2 to 12 hours.
8. Remove the gelato mixture from the refrigerator and whisk it a few times.
9. After installing it, pour the gelato mixture into the ice cream maker bowl.
10. Press the start and gelato buttons while the machine is connected.
11. After the cycle is complete, either serve the gelato immediately away or move it to a freezer-safe, airtight container. It will be a creamy, silky gelato. Before serving, let the gelato freeze for at least two hours if you prefer a firmer texture.

Prep

- Kcal 511, fat 17 g, carbs 85 g

98. Caramel Gelato

Ingredients

- 7 oz whole milk
- 8 oz heavy cream
- 5 ml salt
- 7 egg yolks
- 8 oz granulated sugar.
- 4 oz caramel

Directions

1. According to the manufacturer's recommendations, freeze the ice cream machine bowl for 12 to 24 hours.
2. While waiting, reheat the milk and heavy cream in a saucepan over low heat. The mixture should gradually boil for 15 to 20 minutes. Set aside.
3. Over the egg yolks and sugar that have been beaten in another bowl, pour the heated milk mixture. Continue whisking so you don't wind up burning the egg yolks.
4. Reheat the entire mixture over low heat until it thickens and becomes creamy. Refill the pot with the mixture. The mixture is done when the back of a spoon is coated with it.
5. To remove any cooked egg yolk fragments, strain the gelato base through a fine-mesh sieve into a clean basin, preferably one with a spout.
6. In a separate bowl, mix the salt and the caramel. Pour it into the gelato's base.
7. After being wrapped in plastic wrap, the mixture should cool in the refrigerator for at least 2 to 12 hours.
8. Remove the gelato mixture from the refrigerator and whisk it a few times.
9. After installing it, pour the gelato mixture into the ice cream maker bowl.
10. While the machine is connected, press the start and gelato buttons.
11. After the cycle is finished, either serve the gelato right away or transfer it to an airtight, freezer-safe container. It'll be a smooth, creamy gelato. If you like a firmer texture, freeze the gelato for at least two hours prior to serving.

Prep

- Kcal 496, fat 24 g, carbs 64 g

Ingredients

- 8 oz whole milk
- 14-ounce can sweeten condensed milk
- 2 oz heavy cream
- 2 teaspoons vanilla extract
- 8 oz pitted and chopped fresh cherries.
- 2 oz almonds, roughly chopped
- 30 ml cherry liquor

Directions

1. According to the manufacturer's recommendations, freeze the ice cream machine bowl for 12 to 24 hours.
2. Whole milk, condensed milk, heavy cream, vanilla extract, and cherry liqueur should all be combined in a big bowl at this point. Until everything is smooth and mixed, whisk.
3. For at least 2 to 12 hours, wrap the mixture in plastic wrap and place it in the refrigerator to cool.
4. Take the gelato mixture out of the fridge and give it a couple stirs.
5. Pour the mixture into the bowl of the frozen ice cream maker.
6. Press the start and gelato buttons while the machine is connected.
7. Add the chopped cherries and almonds into the gelato gradually as it is being churned, around 5 to 6 minutes before it is finished.
8. After the cycle is complete, either serve the gelato immediately away or move it to a freezer-safe, airtight container. It will be a creamy, silky gelato. Before serving, let the gelato freeze for at least two hours if you prefer a firmer texture.

Prep

- Kcal 443, fat 20 g, carbs 65 g

- Makes about 4 cups (4 oz per serving)

Ingredients

- 7 oz whole milk
- 8 oz heavy cream
- four oz granulated sugar
- 4 egg yolks
- 5 ml vanilla extract
- 6 tablespoons chocolate hazelnut spread like Nutella.

Directions

1. Freeze the ice cream maker bowl for 12 to 24 hours in accordance with the manufacturer's instructions.
2. Meanwhile, warm the heavy cream, sugar, and whole milk in a saucepan over medium heat. The mixture should gradually boil for 15 to 20 minutes. Set aside.
3. Add the egg yolks to a spotless bowl and stir. To temper the egg yolks and prevent scrambled eggs, begin slowly incorporating the warm milk mixture.
4. Reheat the mixture over low heat until it thickens and becomes creamy. Refill the pot with the mixture. The mixture is done when the back of a spoon is coated with it.
5. Eliminate the heat. After that, incorporate the chocolate hazelnut spread and vanilla bean paste. Blend very well indeed.
6. After being wrapped in plastic wrap, the mixture should cool in the refrigerator for at least 2 to 12 hours.
7. While waiting, chop the hazelnuts and toast them for about 2-3 minutes over medium heat, stirring often in a nonstick frying pan. Set aside for a future objective.
8. Remove the gelato mixture from the refrigerator and whisk it a few times.
9. After assembling the ice cream maker, pour the contents into the bowl.
10. While the machine is connected, press the start and gelato buttons.
11. After the cycle is finished, either serve the gelato right away or transfer it to an airtight, freezer-safe container. It'll be a smooth, creamy gelato. If you like a firmer texture, freeze the gelato for at least two hours prior to serving.

Prep

Kcal 529, fat 34.3 g, carbs 48.7 g,

Measurement Conversion Chart

WEIGHT

IMPERIAL	METRIC
1/2 oz	15 g
1 oz	29 g
2 oz	57 g
3 oz	85 g
4 oz	113 g
5 oz	141 g
6 oz	170 g
8 oz	227 g
10 oz	283 g
12 oz	340 g
13 oz	369 g
14 oz	397 g
15 oz	425 g
1 lb	453 g

MEASUREMENT

CUP	ONCES	MILLILITERS	TABLESPOONS
8 cup	64 oz	1895 ml	128
6 cup	48 oz	1420 ml	96
5 cup	40 oz	1180 ml	80
4 cup	32 oz	960 ml	64
2 cup	16 oz	480 ml	32
1 cup	8 oz	240 ml	16
3/4 cup	6 oz	177 ml	12
2/3 cup	5 oz	158 ml	11
1/2 cup	4 oz	118 ml	8
3/8 cup	3 oz	90 ml	6
1/3 cup	2.5 oz	79 ml	5.5
1/4 cup	2 oz	59 ml	4
1/8 cup	1 oz	30 ml	3
1/16 cup	1/2 oz	15 ml	1

TEMPERATURE

FARENHEIT	CELSIUS
100 °F	37 °C
150 °F	65 °C
200 °F	93 °C
250 °F	121 °C
300 °F	150 °C
325 °F	160 °C
350 °F	180 °C
375 °F	190 °C
400 °F	200 °C
425 °F	220 °C
450 °F	230 °C
500 °F	260 °C
525 °F	274 °C
550 °F	288 °C

Video with execution and how to use Ninja Creami

Homemade Coffee Ice Cream: https://youtu.be/bZCIWFurc9U

Pistachio Gelato Recipe: https://youtu.be/76HDuYk5pGE

17 Easy Milkshake Recipes: https://youtu.be/aPDhAHc_eX0

Ninja Creami: How to Use It and What to Expect | Beginners Guide:
https://youtu.be/ExDFofa2mcM

Conclusion

Using a Ninja blender to make ice cream is entertaining and healthier.

Permit yourself to love your inner meal planner. I concur that preparing smoothies the night before can help you save a lot of time. The blade assembly should never be stored with smoothies, though, since some foods containing active chemicals can lead to pressure buildup and harm. Instead, keep them with Sip & Seal Lids.

The Ninja machine is great for swiftly making nutritious sorbet, frozen yogurt, and ice cream. Finding your favorite recipes requires trial and error, but once you do, it's amazing to make your ice cream at home with a little mess.

It takes some practice to create your recipes, and I've discovered that while it takes some practice to get the ideal settings for handcrafted ice cream tastes, once you do, it's amazing.

You need to be patient. This is not an instant ice cream maker because the ingredients must be frozen twenty-four hours before being poured into the machine.

Made in the USA
Las Vegas, NV
06 August 2023

75711967R00063